Belair Early Years
Our World

Kathy Alcock

Acknowledgements

The author and the publisher would like to thank the following for their invaluable help and support during the preparation of this book:

Amanda Symonds	Helen McMorrow	Shelagh Hughes
Carol Thurman	Isabelle Dillon	Stephen Scoffham
Chris Alcock	Janet Parrett	Stuart Alcock
Christine Laxton	Jill Marsh	Sue Birbeck
Debbie Galley-Buxton	John Collar	Sue Brown
Denise Hill	Laura Christie	Sue Smith
Elizabeth Barber	Lynne Gibbon	Sue Woolgar
Elizabeth Crosson	Marc Barber	Tina Wallace
Fiona Johnston	Mary Letham	Tracy Green
Hania Myers	Nicola Hooper	Victor Parrett
Hardip Banger	Philip Alcock	Warren Harrison
Heather Woodcock	Sarah Newbrook	

Thank you also to the children, students and parents in the following:

Abbey Pre-School	South Deal Primary School
Archers Court School	St Mary's C.E.P. School
Canterbury Christ Church University College	The Parochial School
Hamilton School	Umbrella Pre-school
River C.P. School	Warden House School
Sandwich Infants School	Whitfield Community Playgroup

Published by Collins, An imprint of HarperCollins*Publishers*
77 – 85 Fulham Palace Road, Hammersmith, London, W6 8JB

Browse the complete Collins catalogue at
www.collinseducation.com

© HarperCollins*Publishers* Limited 2012
Previously published in 2007 by Folens
First published in 2001 by Belair Publications

10 9 8 7 6 5 4 3 2 1

ISBN-13 978-0-00-744790-9

Kathy Alcock asserts her moral rights to be identified as the author of this work

British Library Cataloguing in Publication Data
A Catalogue record for this publication is available from the British Library

All Early learning goals, Areas of learning and development, and Aspects of learning quoted in this book are taken from the *Statutory Framework for the Early Years Foundation Stage*, Department for Education, 2012 (available at www.education.gov.uk/publications). This information is licensed under the terms of the Open Government Licence (www.nationalarchives.gov.uk/doc/open-government-licence).

Every effort has been made to trace copyright holders and to obtain their permission for the use of copyright material. The authors and publishers will gladly receive any information enabling them to rectify any error or omission in subsequent editions.

Cover concept: Mount Deluxe   Cover design: Linda Miles, Lodestone Publishing
Cover photography: Nigel Meager   Editor: Elizabeth Miles
Page layout: Ed Gallagher
Photography: Kelvin Freeman, Steve Harrison and Canterbury Christ Church College

Printed and bound by Printing Express Limited, Hong Kong

MIX
Paper from
responsible sources
FSC
www.fsc.org   FSC™ C007454

Contents

Introduction 4

Through the window 6

Over the rainbow 8

Out and about 10

Out for a walk 12

How we travel around 14

Over land and sea 16

Reasons why we travel 18

Let's communicate 20

How we communicate 22

Who will you ring? 24

Whatever the weather 26

What's the weather like today? 28

The seasons 30

All the year round 32

Hot and cold places 34

Dough corner and clay square 36

Clay displays and collections 38

On the farm 40

The world of fairy tales 42

Compass town 46

The street where you live 48

The world where we live 50

Where in the world? 52

Where should we go? 54

Far and away places 56

Jobs people do 58

In the park 60

Action songs and rhymes 62

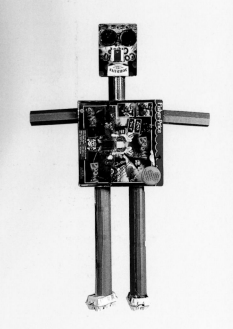

Introduction

The *Belair Early Years* series has been well-loved by early years educators working with the under-fives for many years. This re-launched edition of these practical resource books offers popular, tried and tested ideas, all written by professionals working in early years education. The inspirational ideas will support educators in delivering the three characteristics of effective teaching and learning identified in the Statutory Framework for the Early Years Foundation Stage 2012: playing and exploring, active learning, and creating and thinking critically.

The guiding principles at the heart of the EYFS Framework 2012 emphasise the importance of the unique child, the impact of positive relationships and enabling environments on children's learning and development, and that children develop and learn in different ways and at different rates. The 'hands on' activities in *Belair Early Years* fit this ethos perfectly and are ideal for developing the EYFS prime areas of learning (Communication and language, Physical development, Personal, social and emotional development) and specific areas of learning (Literacy, Mathematics, Understanding the world, Expressive arts and design) which should be implemented through a mix of child-initiated and adult-led activities. Purposeful play is vital for children's development, whether leading their own play or participating in play guided by adults.

Throughout this book full-colour photography is used to offer inspiration for presenting and developing children's individual work with creative display ideas for each theme. Display is highly beneficial as a stimulus for further exploration, as well as providing a visual communication of ideas and a creative record of children's learning journeys. In addition to descriptions of the activities, each theme in this book provides clear Learning Intentions and extension ideas and activities as Home Links to involve parents/carers in their child's learning.

This title, *Our World*, particularly supports children's progress towards attaining the Early Learning Goals in the Understanding the world and Expressive arts and design areas of learning. For young children, the variety within the human and the natural world can cause confusions. Their experiences are limited but even within their first few years of life, children meet large numbers of different people and some children will visit a wide variety of different places through everyday experiences. This book demonstrates ways in which these experiences can be built upon to provide relevant, stimulating, interesting and enjoyable activities to enable children to 'make sense' of the world around them. This will help to provide a secure base from which children's later work in science, design and technology, history, geography and ICT can develop knowledge, skills and understanding.

By using the approaches and activities in this book, practitioners will help children to learn to:
- **explore and develop their natural sense of curiosity**
- **ask questions to find out more about things that interest them**
- **make choices and try out new ideas for investigations**
- **be resilient and try different approaches to problem-solving when ideas don't work**
- **describe their observations and communicate their ideas clearly to others.**

Most significantly, the activities will stimulate children's imagination and encourage a sense of wonder in their new discoveries about the world around them.

I hope that adults and children alike will enjoy exploring the activities in this book.

Kathy Alcock

USING THE ACTIVITIES

This book includes a variety of features to support practitioners using the activities.

Talk about questions

Each of the themes in this book includes suggestions of carefully framed 'Questions to ask' and appropriate 'Language development' pointers for vocabulary you should be aiming to build with children. Children learn by hearing new words and imitating adults, so each of the themes supports how adults should interact with children, including modelling the behaviour you want them to learn.

Outdoor activities and local visits

Using the outdoor environment is an essential part of the Early Years Foundation Stage. This book includes exciting ideas for providing outdoor experiences that are on a large scale such as construction and mapping and how to extend the outdoor activities during indoor play.

TALK ABOUT	
Questions to ask	**Language development**
What does this picture show?	Encourage the children to:
Where is it?	name features
What are the people doing?	describe activities
What do you like/ dislike about this place?	pass opinions

IMPORTANT NOTE

All the following activities could take place in a rural or urban environment, nearby or further afield. It is essential when taking children out of doors that an appropriate adult/children ratio is achieved. All adult helpers must be suitably prepared in advance to ensure maximum learning from the experience.

An excellent way of providing opportunities for children to gather information about the world around them is to take them on visits within the local environment. In this book you will find ideas about what to do before, during and after visits in order to maximise the potential learning that can take place. Sometimes you will need to give the children information prior to visits, for example on how to behave to ensure safety or how to use equipment. Try to avoid pre-empting what they are going to see to avoid stifling investigation of reducing their sense of wonder when a discovery is made. Important notes on safety issues are flagged where appropriate.

Resources you will need

Prior to starting any activity, careful consideration should be given to the provision of and access to resources. Children learn by 'doing things', so should be encouraged to work with a wide range of materials. The resources that you will need for each of the suggested activities are identified at the beginning of each theme.

YOU WILL NEED
- Modelling clay, dough or plasticine
- Rolling pins
- Paint
- Card
- Objects to put in shops
- Biscuits

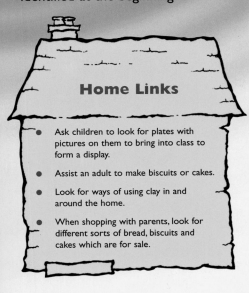

Home Links

- Ask children to look for plates with pictures on them to bring into class to form a display.
- Assist an adult to make biscuits or cakes.
- Look for ways of using clay in and around the home.
- When shopping with parents, look for different sorts of bread, biscuits and cakes which are for sale.

Developing home links

It is important to build partnerships with parents and carers to share information on children's development and encourage parents to use their own knowledge to extend children's experiences of the world. Ideas of how parents might support the children's learning are included as Home Links.

The author believes that the greatest resource any teacher or worker with early years children has is their own imagination. The ideas in this book are designed to stimulate your imagination.

Through the window

LEARNING INTENTIONS

Children will:

- express their ideas pictorially;

- increase their awareness of the features surrounding their school;

- look at the work of famous artists.

YOU WILL NEED

- paint mixed for each colour of the rainbow

- different size brushes

- sugar paper to make window frames

- large pieces of white paper

- pictures of the works of famous artists

STARTING POINTS

- Go for a walk in the local area and talk about the buildings and natural features. Take photographs of features using a digital or Polaroid camera.

- Ask the children to name features they can see through the window.

- Paint pictures of what they can see out of the window, in the playground or park or inside. Take photographs of the actual scene and display near the children's paintings.

- Display paintings by famous artists.

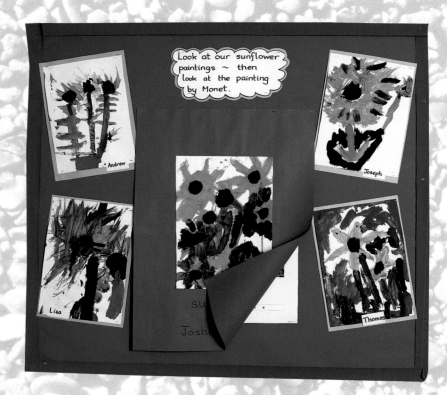

Look at our sunflower paintings ~ then look at the painting by Monet.

Activities

- Look at the work of a famous artist. Talk about what the picture shows and the techniques used. Ask questions such as: 'What does this painting show?' 'What shapes can you see?' 'What colours has the artist used?'

- Display the children's paintings next to or over the originals to create a 'lift the flap' effect. The work of art used here is Van Gogh's 'Sunflowers'.

- Ask children to paint in a particular style, for example using coloured dots, or soaking sugar paper with clear water then dropping spots of coloured paint on the wet paper, using pastels.

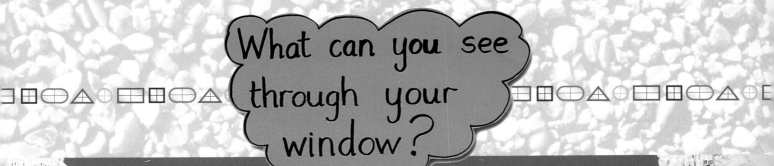

What can you see through your window?

Jessica

A house and some flowers

Oliver W.

Birds flying

I can see the sun

Lauren

Paris

A big house

I can see the trees

I can see a garden

Sarah

Activities

- Make a list of all the things the children can see.

- Provide an outline picture showing the scene children can see from the window. Children add details using their own observations. Make labels for some of the features such as house, garden, tree, sky, road, path, post box. Children attach these labels to the features on the picture.

- Play a simplified version of the game 'I spy …' for example: 'I spy something which leaves grow on …'

Questions to ask

What can you see?
What is behind the …?
What is in front of the …?
Can you describe where … is?
I spy ….

Language development

Children name features.
Position language:- *behind, above, beyond, next to, right, left, in front of, beside, across.*

Activities

- 👋 Look at a rainbow when it appears in the sky or a picture of a rainbow.
- 👋 Teach the children seven colours.
- 👋 Ask them to paint their own picture of a rainbow.

red orange yellow green blue indigo violet

Children can use thick brushes, or thin brushes, or fingers. Ask them which they think is most effective.

Richard

Of

York

Gained

Battle

In

Vain

Activities

👋 Make a giant class rainbow. This could go over a door as in the photograph.

👋 A giant class rainbow could be the centrepiece of a display of objects relating to a theme such as food, for example, you may have a red apple, an orange, a yellow lemon, a green lettuce, a blue box of biscuits, an indigo plum, a violet packet of sweets. Other themes may include clothes, the weather, animals, toys, objects found in the garden, objects found in the street.

👋 Create a group or class poem on the theme.

Home Links

● Ask parents to contribute to the rainbow display by providing coloured objects.

● Ask parents to encourage their children to look for rainbow colours when they are out and about.

Out and about

LEARNING INTENTIONS

Children will:

- talk about their experiences and increase their awareness of their surroundings;

- increase their awareness of how numbers are used in the environment;

- develop mapwork skills.

STARTING POINTS

- Talk about places and features children pass as they travel to class.

- Use photographs as stimuli in encouraging children to talk about places they have visited with adults.

- Introduce the concept of 'plan view' by making a simple plan of the classroom. Put Velcro on the plan and on the furniture. Children have to place the pieces in the right place.

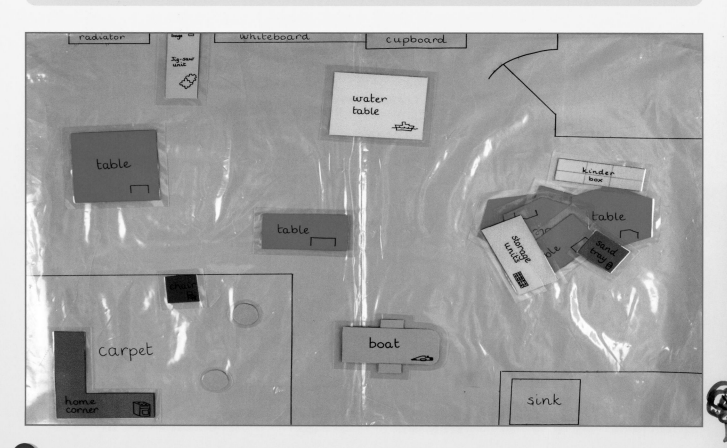

We park the car here

I could call my mum from here

I had my party here

People post letters to friends

We can buy stamps here

Before the visit

Identify a place to be visited such as a local park, play area or place of worship. Talk about what the children know already about it. Look at a photograph of what it looks like now and if possible, in the past so changes can be identified. Look at the place on a large-scale map or an aerial photograph.

Prepare speech bubbles to be completed after the visit.

Adults work with children to compile a list of questions to be answered before and during the visit.

Our questions ?

What is the place called?
Who lives there?
What do people do there?
What buildings are there?
Is it a safe place?
What should people not do there?
What do we like/dislike about the place?

Out for a walk

During the visit

- On the journey, children identify features by completing an 'I have seen…' tally chart.

- During a walk children collect items in a small pot or bag. These can be sorted and displayed on return. (Note: supervise carefully.)

- Stop to take photographs of places children find interesting.

- Play 'I spy' using signs and symbols as well as other easily identified features.

- Children choose a building such as a shop or a house or a feature such as a gate or a bridge and make a close observation by talking into a small portable tape recorder. Photographs of these can be taken and made into a collection. Children listen to the recordings and identify and match to the pictures.

- Ask children to draw or talk about what they can see in front and behind them, or looking down or looking up. North and South may be introduced.

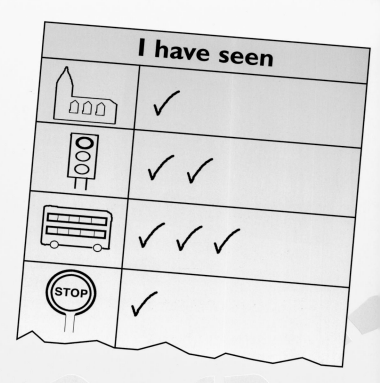

After the visit

- Ask children to identify key features and the route followed on a simple uncomplicated, large-scale map.

- Prepare speech bubbles from card. Children dictate to an adult their comments about places they have visited. Add these to the photographs (see page 11) or to the map display.

- Make signs and symbols for use in the classroom.

- Compare pictures taken of the same place during a different season to look for differences and similarities.

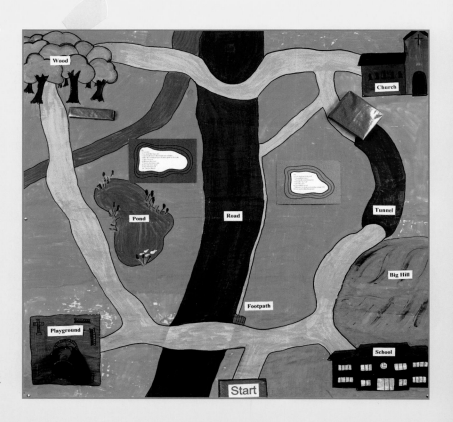

Did you see?

hill

church

river

railway

bridge

Looking for numbers

✋ Make signs and symbols that you have seen on the visit which use numbers to give information. These may include road signs, dates on buildings, times when cars can be parked and for how long, prices of goods, opening times, car registration numbers.

✋ Make your own versions of these to give information to the children such as opening times for the class shop, prices of food in the class café, the number of children allowed in the book corner or home corner at any one time.

Activities

✋ Make a simple symbols chart with a mixture of features they did and did not see. Can the children remember what they saw and where they saw it?

Home Links

● Ask children to talk to adults at home about a visit undertaken.

● Collect pictures of places they would like to find out about.

● Make a car number plate of their own or another car.

● Play number games with the numbers on the plate e.g., add two numbers, order them from largest to smallest.

How we travel around

LEARNING INTENTIONS

Children will:

- distinguish between different forms of transport;
- begin to understand the processes involved in making a journey;
- ask questions about how people travel.

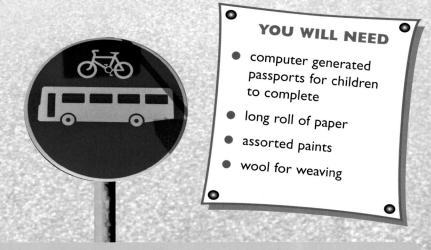

YOU WILL NEED

- computer generated passports for children to complete
- long roll of paper
- assorted paints
- wool for weaving

STARTING POINTS

- Read a story to the children which involves various vehicles and methods of travelling such as one of the Postman Pat, Thomas the Tank Engine or Gumdrop series.
- Visit a train, bus or coach station or an airport.
- Watch vehicles passing the building where you are working. Complete a traffic count.
- A child recounts a journey they have made recently.
- Sing songs such as 'Here comes a big red bus' and 'The Wheels on the Bus'.
- Read 'The Owl and the Pussy Cat' poem by Edward Lear.

ACTIVITIES

- Bring in examples of passports. Talk about why people have passports, why they are used and what information they include.
- Make a passport and go on a pretend journey abroad. Use the 'magic carpet' or 'all aboard the aeroplane' idea.
- Provide tasks for the 'pretend journey' such as:
    - Make a place name sign.
    - Make a menu for the café.
    - Make tickets for the journey.
    - Make sound effects for the journey using instruments.

BY FOOT

Activities

✋ Children can make footprints along a long roll of paper.

✋ Paint the bottom of their feet.

✋ Carefully supervise them creating footprints.

✋ Talk to the children about when they might walk on a journey.

✋ Think about safety.

CROSSING THE ROAD

DO:
stop at the kerb
find an adult
look both ways

DO NOT:
run across the road
stop on the road
play on the road

Activities

✋ Make footprint instructions.

This can be done in different ways for younger and older children. For children who can read numbers use arrows and numbers e.g., walk forward three paces, right two paces.
For other children use symbols like dots or footprints.

Over land and sea

Activities

- 🖐 Children paint pictures of journeys across water.
- 🖐 They could weave wool around the edges of the boat or land in the distance as in this example.
- 🖐 Talk about where passengers are going and what luggage they would take with them.
- 🖐 Look at a timetable, make and buy tickets.
- 🖐 Think of other vehicles that people use and why e.g., buses and cars

BY BOAT

BY TRAIN

Ask the children to act out a journey. Together adults and children create and set out the scene. This could be a train. Children take turns to assume the role of driver, wearing appropriate hat or uniform.

have trave
by bus

BY BUS

Home Links

- Cut out pictures of different vehicles and make a 'How we travel' zig-zag book.

- Ask parents to take a photograph of their child in front of the mode of transport they use when going on a journey.

Questions to ask

Where are you going?
How will you travel?
How long will it take?
When might you travel by bus? plane? train? car?

Language development

Holiday, visit, shopping, walk, train, bus, plane, hour, day, long time, town, city, names of places e.g., Spain, London, shopping centre, supermarket.

Reasons why we travel

CLASS SURVEY

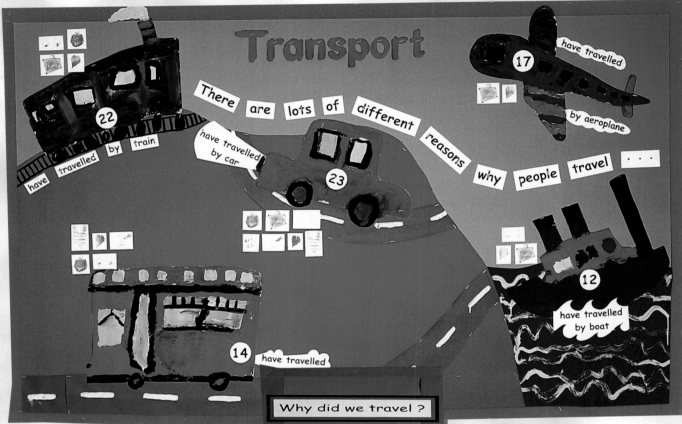

Transport

There are lots of different reasons why people travel . . .

22 have travelled by train

have travelled by car

23

17 have travelled by aeroplane

12 have travelled by boat

14 have travelled

Why did we travel ?

Shopping
School
Holiday
Ballet class
Visit family
Football
Swimming
Sight seeing

KEY

Asking questions

Who has travelled by car, (bus, plane, boat)?
Why have you travelled by car, (bus, plane, boat)?
Which is the best way to travel if you are going:
on holiday?
to the shops?
to London?
to Sydney?
to New York?

Activities

- Make a simple block graph to show how many children have travelled on the different forms of transport.

- Alternatively put the number of children on the form of transport as in the collage above.

- Ask the children to draw a picture that represents the reason they travelled. Use these as a symbol key for the large collage.

Labels visible in display:
Police Car · Ambulance · Fire Engine · Steering Wheel · Car · Lights · Wheel · Bumper · Hub-Cap · Exhaust Pipe · Lorry · Tyre · Van

Activities

Talk about different types of journeys people make and what luggage they take with them.

Provide a collection of toy vehicles to be sorted into different categories by colour, size, type and what they travel on.

Make a display of vehicles with labels and enquiry questions such as:

What is this?
Where does this travel?
Who travels in this?
How is this used?
How many people could travel in this car?
Where is this bus going to stop?
What is the name of the train station?
Where does the plane fly?
Who travels in a plane?

When children play with toy vehicles, adults talk to them about the scenarios they are creating. Ask questions such as:

When your car crashed why do you think that happened?
Are the people in the coach wearing seat belts?
Where will the ambulance be going?
What is going to happen next?
Where is it safe to cross the road?

Let's communicate

LEARNING INTENTIONS

Children will:

- develop an understanding of communicating for a specific purpose;
- increase awareness of work in a post office;
- engage in role-play.

Miss Polly had a dolly

Miss Polly had a dolly who was sick, sick, sick.
So she called for the doctor to be quick, quick, quick.
The doctor came with his bag and his hat.
And he knocked at the door with a rat-a-tat-tat.

He looked at the dolly and he shook his head,
He said 'Miss Polly, put her straight to bed'.
He wrote on a paper for a pill, pill, pill,
"I'll be back in the morning with my bill, bill, bill."

YOU WILL NEED

- writing materials
- huge box
- paint
- telephones
- office stationery
- sugar paper
- pictures and objects to represent people to call e.g., Lego people.

STARTING POINTS

- Visit a post office where people are working using office equipment.
- Read a story or an information book about one of the emergency services and talk about the work they do and how we communicate with them.
- Sing a song such as 'Miss Polly had a dolly'. (See above.)
- Ask questions such as: 'Why do you use a telephone or fax machine?' 'How do you make a telephone call and what happens?' 'Make and receive a telephone call, a fax message and an email.'

Activities

- Talk about how we communicate with people who do not live nearby.
- Write a letter.
- Make a telephone box in an outdoor area.

Asking questions

Who will you write to?
Where do they live?
What will you write?

What goes on the envelope?

Language development

Names of people they know.
Names of places.
Talk about reasons for writing e.g., Thank you, Birthdays.
Name, address, stamp.

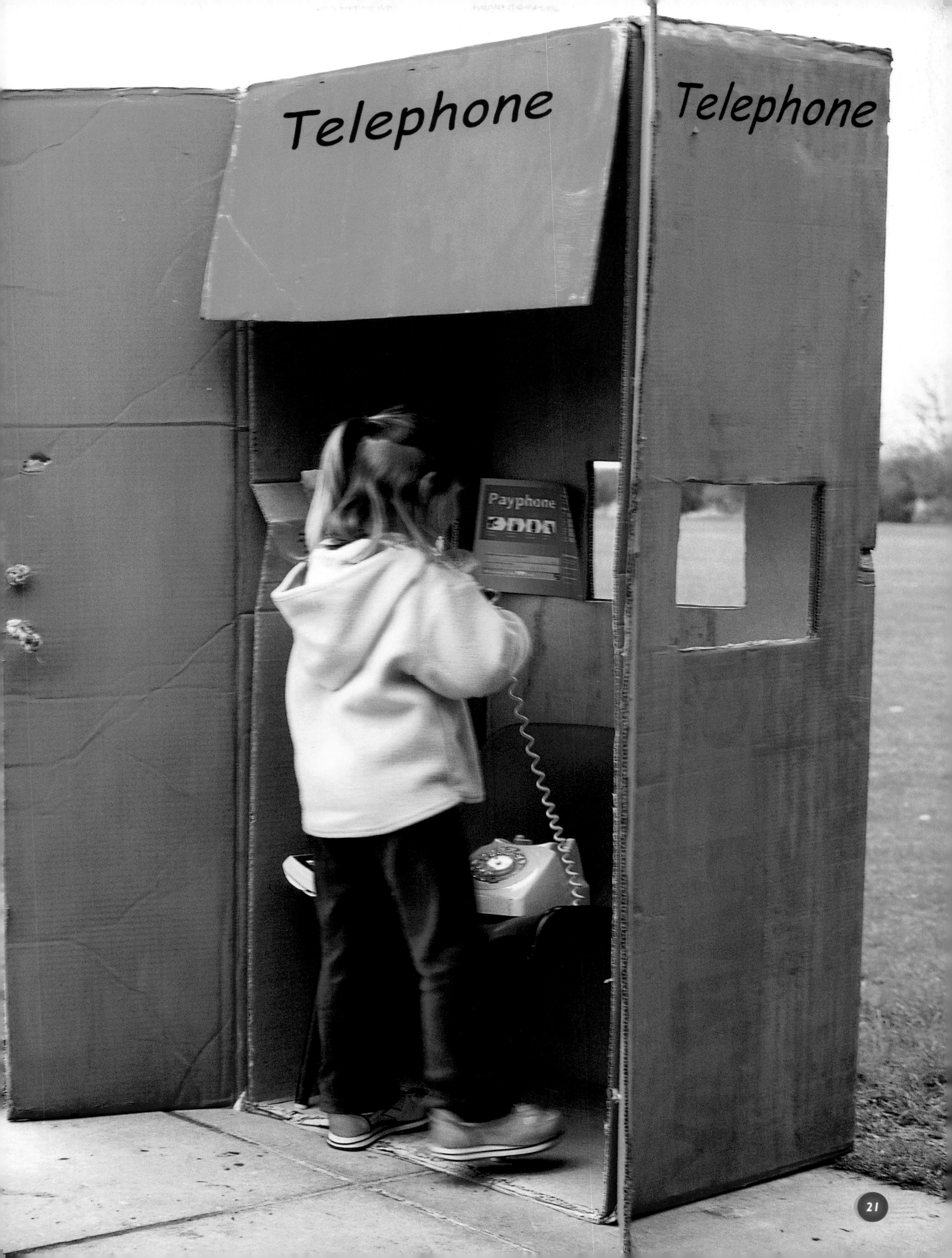
Telephone
Telephone
Payphone

How we communicate

SET UP A POST OFFICE

Activities

✋ Read 'The Jolly Postman' and the 'Jolly Post Office'.

✋ Talk to the children about why we need post offices, what services they provide and the jobs people do in them.

✋ Set up a role play corner - children can play different roles such as postal workers or customers.

✋ Make labels for the post office.

✋ Make a post box with times of collection displayed.

✋ Parcels and letters should have local and more distant addresses.

✋ Make a sorting box with four local streets labelled.

✋ Children can sort the letters to be delivered to the four streets.

✋ Make some car tax discs. These can be computer generated by scanning some in.

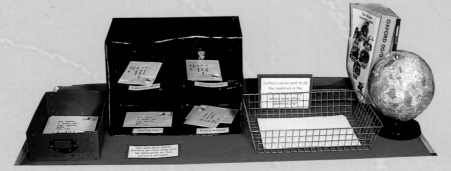

From over the hills and far away ....

..a jolly postman came one day

Spring 2001

How do you send messages to someone who is far away? Do you use the telephone? Do you use e-mail? Do you write letters?

telephone

letter

internet

How do we communicate with people who are a long way away?

signs and signals

fax

Telephones work by sending the messages along wires, which either go under the ground, or overhead attached to wooden poles.

E-mail and the internet work by using the telephone lines as well.

Letters are posted in the post box. They are then collected and taken to the sorting office where they are sent to the town on the address. The postmen and women there deliver the letters to the houses.

Activities

- Ask the children to list all the ways we communicate with people further away for example letter, email, fax, telephone, internet.

- Make a display generated by the ideas in the books.

- Make a display of different types and sizes of letters and parcels, email and faxes.

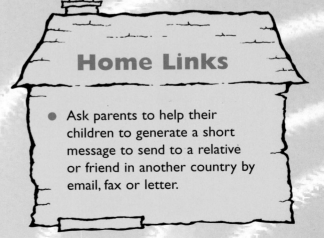

Home Links

- Ask parents to help their children to generate a short message to send to a relative or friend in another country by email, fax or letter.

Who will you ring?

Activities

👋 Make a giant telephone to use in an interactive display. Create the numbers using materials, which give a tactile effect of spots for counting.

👋 Explain to the children what an emergency call is, how to make the call and when the emergency number should be dialled and when not to dial it.

👋 Use the display to introduce other services which can be contacted by telephone such as a library, shops, schools, post offices, garages, banks, doctors. Talk with the children about what services each provides and where the nearest ones are found.

👋 Add instructions and labels to the telephone display such as:

- Pick up the receiver.
- Hold one end to your ear and the other to your mouth.
- Dial the emergency number.
- Wait for an answer.
- Ask for the service you need.
- Give your name and address.
- Say what the problem is.

Activities

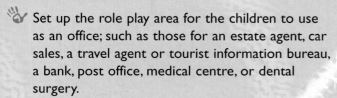 Set up the role play area for the children to use as an office; such as those for an estate agent, car sales, a travel agent or tourist information bureau, a bank, post office, medical centre, or dental surgery.

Equip the office with computer, model and discarded telephones, fax machines and other office equipment with which children experiment. Provide paper, envelopes and different types of writing equipment as well as a waste paper and recycling bin.

Provide a set of task cards relating to the type of area you have set up such as: 'Buy a new house' 'Book a holiday' 'Change some money into Euros'.

Home Links

● Ask parents to take children to visit one or more of the services you have talked and learned about.

● Prepare a short message to send to a friend in another country by email, telephone or fax.

Whatever the weather

LEARNING INTENTIONS

Children will:

- gain a greater understanding of different weather conditions;
- know that there are seasonal patterns to weather e.g., it is more likely to snow in winter;
- know that some places in the world are cold all the time.

YOU WILL NEED

- tissue paper – different colours
- card tubes (not from toilet rolls) and cardboard
- sugar paper
- cotton wool
- seeds, leaves
- different coloured material
- assorted paints and brushes

Activities

- Cut out the shape of a boy and a girl from cardboard. Provide collections of clothes relating to different types of weather. Fix Velcro to the back of the clothes and in strategic places on the figures. Make title display cards depicting different types of weather.

- Ask the children to dress the boy and the girl appropriately according to the changing weather.

Asking questions

What is the weather like today?

How should we dress the boy and girl today?

Hold up an item. When would you wear this?

What would you wear if the weather was wet, windy etc.?

Language development

Hot, cold, cloudy, raining, snowing, windy.

Warm clothes, clothes to keep cool.

Name items we wear:
in cold weather / in hot weather

Hat, jeans, shorts, gloves etc.

Today it is hot

- Change the display to clothes for special occasions or clothes from around the world.

- Use an overhead projector and transparencies.

- Use non-permanent pens to draw the clothes, colour and design them.

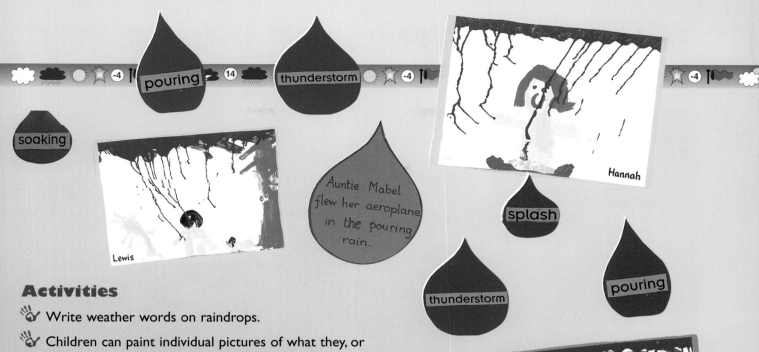

Lewis

Hannah

soaking

pouring

thunderstorm

Auntie Mabel flew her aeroplane in the pouring rain.

splash

thunderstorm

pouring

Activities

👋 Write weather words on raindrops.

👋 Children can paint individual pictures of what they, or people they know, do in different weather conditions.

Story map

👋 Make a story map. An adult draws the outline of the scene to be recreated and children select materials to be used to represent each area and feature in the picture.

👋 Create labels and characters with Velcro on the back which children place on appropriate places on a picture map to retell the story of rain.

splash

Oliver W.

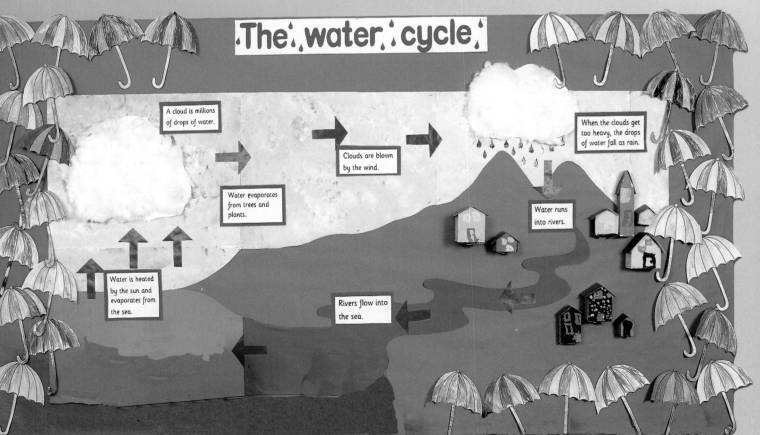

The water cycle

A cloud is millions of drops of water.

Clouds are blown by the wind.

When the clouds get too heavy, the drops of water fall as rain.

Water evaporates from trees and plants.

Water runs into rivers.

Water is heated by the sun and evaporates from the sea.

Rivers flow into the sea.

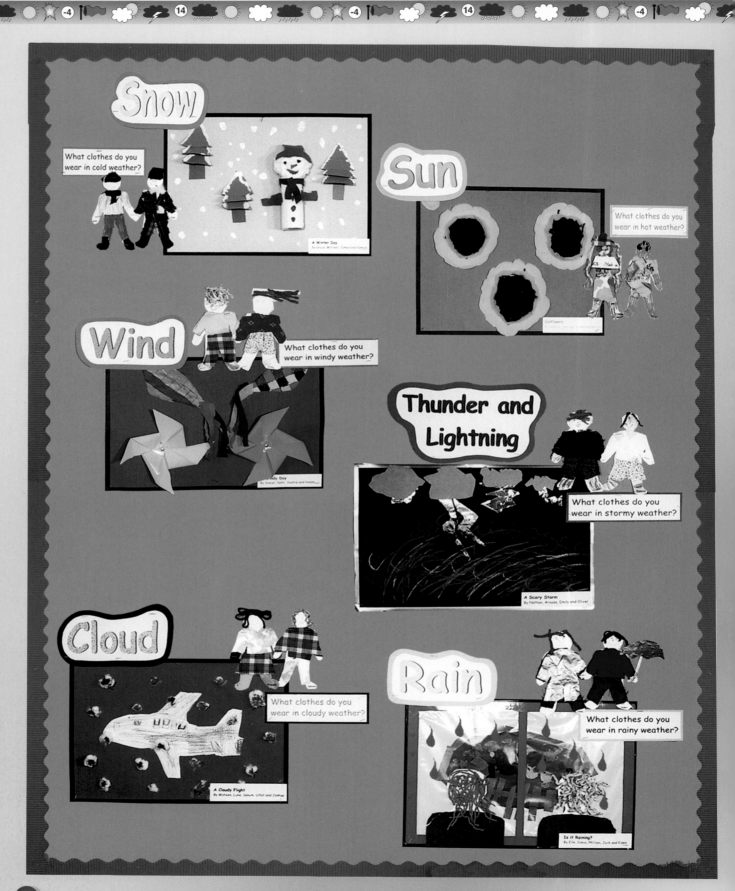

Activities

🖐 Ask the children to draw weather pictures or contribute to a collage.

🖐 Dress the boy and girl appropriately for the weather.

🖐 You could laminate some pictures so that the children can draw on the picture with water-based felt tip pens. The example on page 27 asks children to draw raindrops. These can be wiped off easily with a damp cloth for other children to take a turn.

🖐 Make a large wall display with your weather pictures around a simple map of the whole country.

🖐 Write weather questions on the display for children to answer and talk about.

🖐 Make a range of weather symbols for children to put on the map. One for where they live and for other areas. The children can be encouraged to listen to the weather forecast.

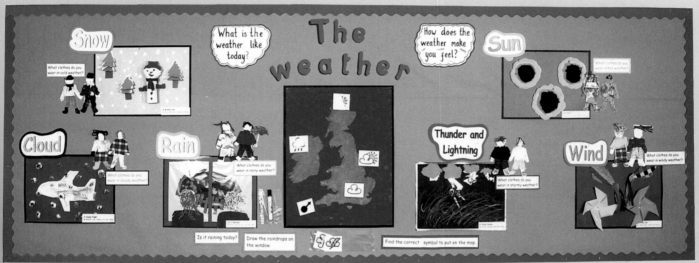

Activities

🖐 Ask the children to write 'weather words' and draw an appropriate picture.

🖐 Make envelopes with the symbols used around the map and use the same words to describe the symbols.

🖐 Children put their words in the envelopes which best describes their weather word eg 'nippy' would go in the envelope labelled 'wind'.

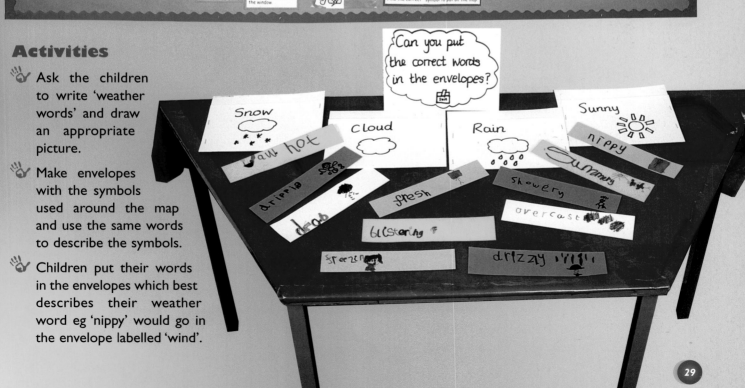

The seasons

Activities

 Share poems about the seasons.

Asking questions	Language development
Do you remember what it was like in winter? summer? autumn? spring? What do we wear in summer, autumn, winter and spring? Why?	Encourage children to think about how seasonal weather affects their lives: Holidays, building snowmen, kicking fallen leaves. Sandals, wellingtons, boots, scarves, coats, T-shirts etc.

Make individual collages which represent the seasons.

For example, the sun to represent summer. Let the children choose the materials and colours they will use.

We used these instructions to make our sun visors.

How to make a sun visor

1. Cut a strip of card 60cm long and about 5cm wide
2. Cut out the peak of the visor by following black lines.
3. Glue peak onto coloured card and cut it out.
4. Fold the peak along the dotted line and staple or sellotape to centre of strip
5. Decorate the sun visor as you like, then sellotape to fit around head.

Daisy's Giant Sunflower
A Lift-the-Flap Book
With Removable Height Chart
Emma Damon

The Seasons

The World of Weather

SUN SNOW STARS SKY

Activities

Make a seasonal collage with the focus on colours which the season represents.

Spring	Represent blossom with shades of pink and white and new plants with shades of green.
Summer	Bright, warm, shiny colours such as yellow, gold, red, orange.
Autumn	Dried leaf and seed collages in brown, orange, russet, ochre.
Winter	Colder, darker shades of blue, grey, black, white, silver.

Add appropriate words to the pictures.

Home Links

- Ask children to bring suitable materials for the collage.

- Collect postcards or photographs of different seasons.

- Encourage the parents to talk about what they do in different seasons e.g., summer holidays.

sunrise summer warm sun shadows sunset

sand

holidays

hot

boiling

The sun has got his hat on,
Hip hip hip hooray!

The sun has got his hat on and he's coming out to play.

Which hat would you choose to wear on a sunny day?

Would any of these hats keep your head dry?

Which hat would keep your head warm?

All the year round

● Use photographs of familiar scenes to depict seasonal change throughout the year. Keep the display up all year and add to it as the year progresses.

Winter

Summer

Spring

Autumn

Summer

● Talk about the changes that take place and how these affect people's lives.

Remember summer can be hot and wet

Summer

Cross-curricular links

A seasonal display can also be used for literacy and numeracy development as in the example below.

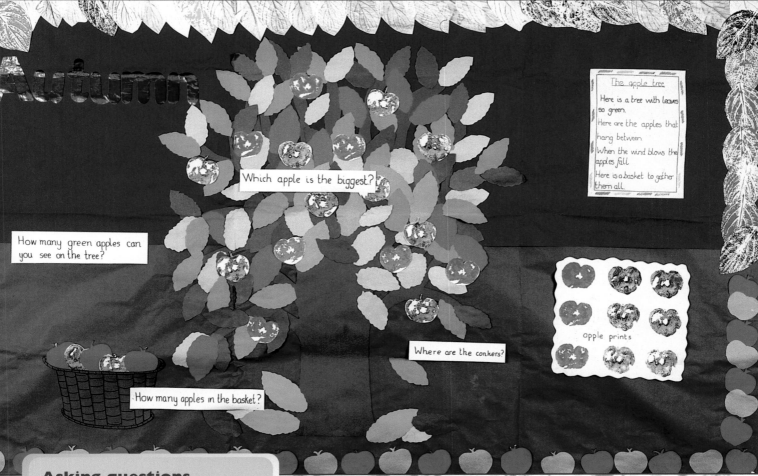

Autumn

The apple tree

Here is a tree with leaves so green.

Here are the apples that hang between

When the wind blows the apples fall

Here is a basket to gather them all.

Which apple is the biggest?

How many green apples can you see on the tree?

Where are the conkers?

How many apples in the basket?

apple prints

Asking questions

What is the weather like now?

How has it changed since Christmas/ beginning of the year etc?

What kind of clothes do we wear in summer/ winter?

When do people go on holiday if they want hot weather?

Language development

Encourage children to use locational words such as:

above, below, next to, beside, nearer, nearest, right, left

Activities

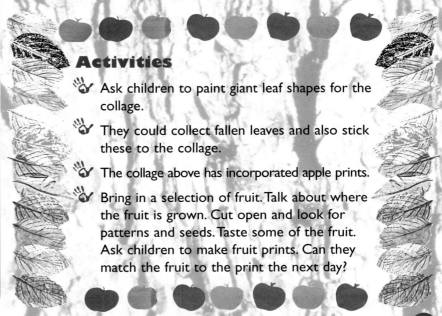

✋ Ask children to paint giant leaf shapes for the collage.

✋ They could collect fallen leaves and also stick these to the collage.

✋ The collage above has incorporated apple prints.

✋ Bring in a selection of fruit. Talk about where the fruit is grown. Cut open and look for patterns and seeds. Taste some of the fruit. Ask children to make fruit prints. Can they match the fruit to the print the next day?

Hot and cold places

Activities

Provide children with a collection of jigsaws related to the theme of seasons. This idea can relate to almost any topic.

Using pictures

Prepare large pictures of a range of locations such as a beach, a funfair, a mountain scene, a snowscape. Ask children to sort a collection of postcards into trays beneath the pictures.

Collect a range of objects used when it is hot. Make labels e.g., sand, sea etc. as shown in the photograph below. Children pick up an object and select the best place for it e.g., flippers next to the label for sea.

waves

sea

water

stones

pebbles

Put the words and objects in the place you may find them

sand

Activities

- 👋 Children can make individual snowmen using cotton wool or tissue paper on tubes.

- 👋 Teach them the rhyme '10 cold snowmen sitting on the wall', to the tune of '10 Green Bottles'.

- 👋 Look at books and pictures of animals in the Artic and Antarctica.

- 👋 Use a globe to show the children where these are. They can make different animals to contribute to a collage.

10 cold snowmen sitting on a wall.

The North Pole

The South Pole

The other name for the North Pole is the Arctic.

The hottest place on the Earth is called the Equator.

Where is the coldest place on Earth?

Penguins live in the South Pole.

Polar bears live in the North Pole.

Where do you think the hottest place is?

The other name for the South Pole is Antarctica.

'Dough corner' and 'clay square'

LEARNING INTENTIONS

Children will:

- discover that some materials come from natural sources but others are made;

- understand that materials are used for different purposes and have different properties;

- handle malleable materials and begin to relate their activity to the 'real world.'

- discover through play that several processes are involved in making products.

STARTING POINTS

- Make a picture map of the nearest shopping street to the school or nursery. Mark on the places where you can buy things made of dough or clay. Are they 'on a corner' or 'in a square' or 'in the middle' of a street?

- Visit a baker's shop or look in the window of a pottery or china shop.

- Bring in a selection of bread, rolls, cakes and biscuits to form a display. Ask children to copy some of these when playing with playdough.

- Display an assortment of pots and plates. Add labels and enquiry questions such as: 'What is this used for?' 'What picture is on this plate?' 'Find out where this was made.'

Activities

Making models

👋 Give children pieces of soft, self-drying clay, Plasticine or playdough and ask them to create their own object. They explain to an adult how they made it and what it should be used for. When dry it can be painted and/or varnished. A label explaining its use should be put near the product on the display table.

👋 Ask children to make a clay name plaque which they decorate and paint.

Manipulating with hands.

Rolling out the clay.

Painting to finish off.

👋 Make a collection of everyday objects. Talk about the materials used to make them. Add shapes made from paper and ask the children to match them to the objects.

Activities

Take photographs and find pictures of things in your area which are made from clay such as chimney pots, roof tiles, flowerpots and vases, name plaques. Display these on a board above a table on which children's own clay creations are placed.

Find pictures in books and on CD Roms showing ways in which clay is used in other countries such as cooking pots, clay ovens, fine china, houses, bricks. Talk about these and add the pictures to the display.

Make a collection of pictures or find actual examples of house, street and village name plaques. Ask questions such as: 'What is this made from?' 'Is it made from clay?' 'How is it decorated?' 'What colours are used?' 'Where is this sign found?'

Bring in an interesting plate. Explain why you like the plate, where it came from or the story behind it. Ask children to bring in a plate from home (or a picture or drawing of one) and tell the story of where it came from and anything interesting they can find out about it.

Collect objects which would be sold in the shops which are found in the picture map (page 36).

Baking

Make biscuits and cakes with different coloured playdough or actual ingredients.

Show children the ingredients used to make bread dough and talk, in simple terms, about the bread making process. Discuss the different sorts of bread you can buy in a shop.

Children make their own roll using prepared dough. This could be taken home with the cooking instructions.

Playdough Recipe - mix in pan. Medium heat until mixture leaves side of pan. Knead. Store in container in fridge.
- Two cups plain flour
- One cup salt
- Two cups water
- Two tablespoons cooking oil
- Two teaspoons cream of tartar
- Add colourings.

Warning! Do not use blue powder paint as it reacts to form a sulphurous gas.

Surveys

Conduct a survey to discover which biscuits or cakes the children like to eat.

Display this information with a small picture or the name of each child in the section showing the picture of their favourite biscuit.

Home Links

- Ask children to look for plates with pictures on them to bring into class to form a display.

- Assist an adult to make biscuits or cakes.

- Look for ways of using clay in and around the home.

- When shopping with parents, look for different sorts of bread, biscuits and cakes which are for sale.

A snail and pot by Megan

A bridge we saw on holiday by Madison - age 3

Name and retol plaque made by students and pre-school children

On the farm

LEARNING INTENTIONS

Children will:

- gain a greater understanding of farm life;
- know where milk comes from;
- know the difference between physical features and human features;
- develop mapwork skills - plan view.

STARTING POINTS

- Look at pictures of rural life.
- Take the children on a visit to an 'open farm' if possible.
- Talk about farm products.
- Sing songs such as 'Old MacDonald had a farm'.

Activities

Story sticks

 Retell a process such as the story of milk.

You could use story sticks. Draw pictures for the children to sequence.

Put a picture of each stage of the process on a stick and hold each up as you 'tell the story'.

For example:

1. The cow is in the field.
2. She eats the grass.
3. The cow makes milk inside her.
4. The farmer takes the cow to be milked.
5. The machine takes the milk from the cow's udder.
6. The milk goes into a big tank.
7. The tanker takes the milk to the dairy where the milk is put into bottles and containers.
8. We buy milk to use for drinking and cooking.

Repeat with another set of story sticks that enable the children to retell another process on the farm e.g. the story of bread or the story of butter.

YOU WILL NEED

- picture sequence of the story of milk
- stories and rhymes about farming
- small pictures of natural features e.g. hill, river, stream
- small pictures of built features e.g. home, road, fence
- coloured card, tissue, paint, shiny paper, glue

The story of milk

Home Links

- Encourage the parents to talk to the children about the processes that take place before the food arrives on the table. Many children when asked 'where does bread come from?' will say 'the shop'.

- Parents can also talk about where the food they eat comes from for example banana plantations in the West Indies, orange groves in Africa etc.

Make a class collage

- Label physical features e.g. rivers, streams, hills.
- Label human features e.g. houses, barns, fences.
- Label animals.
- Write questions on the display as discussion points.

Games to make

Picture / plan matching game
Match the plans of things on the farm to the pictures.
Add labels to the plans.

Physical / human features sorting game
Children put the pictures in the correct set.

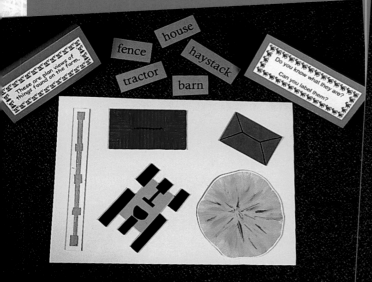

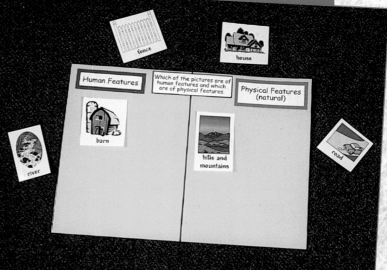

The world of fairy tales

LEARNING INTENTIONS

Children will:

- retell familiar stories.
- make up their own stories and take part in role play with increasing confidence.
- develop mapwork skills.

Using puppets

STARTING POINTS

- The children play with puppets and soft toys.
- Ana adult reads or tells a story to be acted out by the children using puppets.

- Use nursery rhymes and stories that have geographical opportunities e.g., 'Golidlocks and The Three Bears', 'Little Red Riding Hood', 'Mary Had A Little Lamb'.

Activities

Stories and rhymes

Using finger puppets depicting familiar characters, children retell the story or the rhyme such as 'Little Red Riding Hood' or 'Two Little Dicky Birds'.

They make appropriate actions in retelling their story to show movement and use geographical vocabulary as applicable such as: 'up the hill' 'across the river' 'through the town' 'round the roundabout' 'over the sea'.

Match the story titles or rhymes to the sets of finger puppets.

Use puppets to act out a story which children have made up with the help of an adult.

Give each child a toy or a puppet. An adult tells them a story involving a series of actions using their own toy or puppet. The adult then asks the children to carry out a series of instructions using the puppets such as:

1. Go down a road
2. Pass through a gate
3. Climb over a wall
4. Look for a house
5. Go in and up the stairs
6. Find a bed and go to sleep

Draw a picture map of the area where the story takes place. Use locational language.

to

through

over

up

across

along

from

Jack and the Beanstalk

Journeys

Some fairy tales are ideal for developing the children's understanding of journeys and their ability to use locational language.

Locational words

up	down	high	low	in	out
on	under	outside	inside	right	left
to	from	next to	beside	route	over
travel	along	go	arrive	across	cross

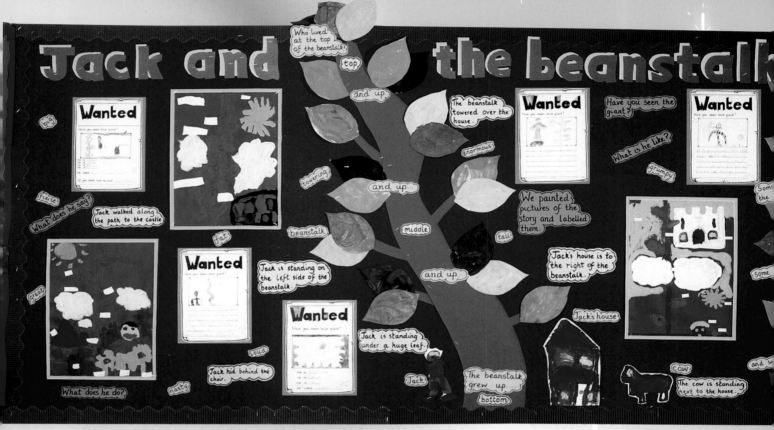

Activities

Tell the story of 'Jack and the Beanstalk'.

Ask the children to describe Jack's home and the Giant's castle

Compare the two homes. Encourage the children to use comparatives such as bigger, smaller, larger, longer.

Talk about the different journeys Jack made:
- to the market,
- up the Beanstalk,
- to the Giant's castle.

Three Billy Goats Gruff

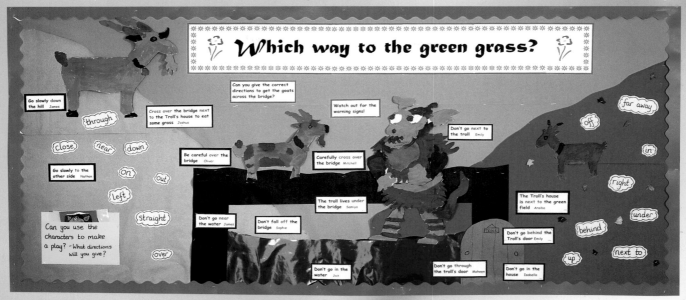

Tell the story of 'Three Billy Goats Gruff'

- Ask the children to use locational words to describe the route the goats take.

- Scribe sentences for the children for the display.

- Make small pictures of the characters so that the children can devise a play.

Hansel and Gretel

Tell the story of 'Hansel and Gretel' *Links with geography and science*

- The display above shows a night scene for the journey the children make.

- Talk about how the children will find their way during the day and at night.

- How could a map help them?

- Make a simple map of the area (as on page 42). Laminate it so children can draw the route with a water-based felt tip pen.

Compass town

LEARNING INTENTIONS

Children will:

- know the various features that make up a town;
- know what services are provided in the town;
- be introduced to north, east, south and west.

STARTING POINTS

- Provide play mats and play maps, homemade and commercially produced, that show roads and rail tracks. These can be used for the children to build on and when playing with toy vehicles. In this way children will learn to follow routes and to build structures in sensible places.

- Play a game such as 'Where does it land?' using something to be rolled on the play mat. Children answer questions such as *Has it landed on a safe place? What feature has it landed on? What would you do there?* This game could be played on a map depicting any environment - country scene, a farm, a large map depicting land and sea.

- Read an information book about the town.

- Play board games, which involve taking turns and moving an object a number of places.

Compass Town board game

- Explain that the children are going to make a game - a pictorial map of an imaginary town.

- Ask the children what buildings they think should go on their game.

- Give them small pieces of paper to draw features of a town.

- Draw roads that run north, east, south and west. Divide the roads into squares and explain to the children that one square equals one move.

- The children should decide where the features should be placed on the board.

- The game can be played at two levels:

Following directions

- Make cards that involve children moving along the board. You can vary the number of instructions according to the ability of the children. You may wish to make a board game that deals only with numbers of less than five for example.

Giving directions

- Make a number of cards that ask the children a direction question.

- Children describe the directions as they move the toy vehicle.

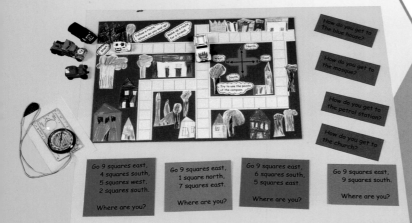

East bound

How do you get to the blue house?

How do you get to the mosque?

How do you get to the petrol station?

How do you get to the church?

Go 9 squares east, 4 squares south, 5 squares west, 2 squares south. Where are you?

Go 9 squares east, 1 square north, 7 squares east. Where are you?

Go 9 squares east, 6 squares south, 5 squares east. Where are you?

Go 9 squares east, 9 squares south. Where are you?

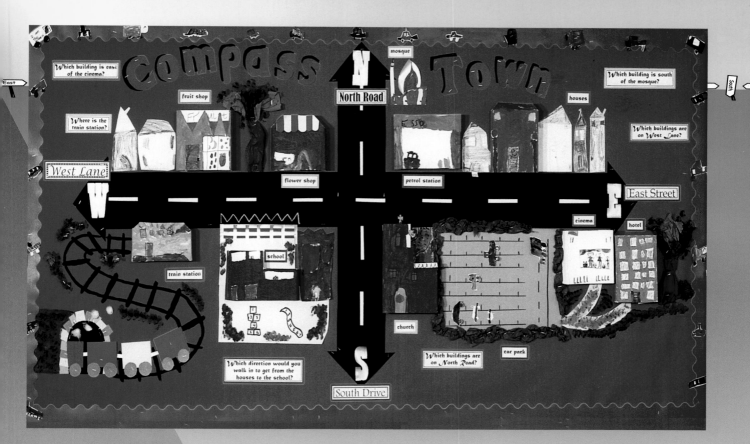

The display board shows:

Compass Town

- North Road (running north-south)
- South Drive
- West Lane
- East Street
- N, S, E, W compass points

Labels on the display: mosque, houses, fruit shop, train station, flower shop, petrol station, school, church, cinema, hotel, car park

Question cards on the display:
- Which building is east of the cinema?
- Where is the train station?
- Which building is south of the mosque?
- Which buildings are on West Lane?
- Which direction would you walk in to get from the houses to the school?
- Which buildings are on North Road?

Activities

- Provide a set of labels with appropriate vocabulary such as *house, road, shop, school, railway station, and car park*. Read the labels with the children and ask them to place the labels in the right place on the class map. Children can use these during undirected play.

- Make small cardboard arrows for the children to use with the class map or on a play mat. They plot a route with the arrows for a friend to follow. Use these using some of the conventions such as *stopping at road junctions, driving on the appropriate side of the road*.

- Children can make up rhymes to help them remember the four compass points:

For example:

Never Eat Shredded Wheat
Naughty Elephants Squirt Water

Naughty
Elephants
Squirt
Water

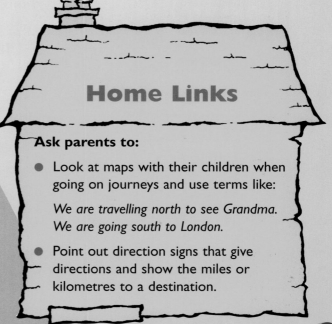

Asking questions

In which direction would you walk to get from the flower shop to the school?

Which buildings are north of West Lane?

In which direction would you drive from the fruit shop to the petrol station?

Home Links

Ask parents to:

- Look at maps with their children when going on journeys and use terms like:

  We are travelling north to see Grandma. We are going south to London.

- Point out direction signs that give directions and show the miles or kilometres to a destination.

The street where you live

LEARNING INTENTIONS

Children will:

- know where they live;

- be able to count and recognise numbers in the environment;

- increase their awareness that numbers are used in a variety of ways to give information;

- understand that different activities take place in the local area;

- know why different street furniture is used.

STARTING POINTS

- Talk to the children about where they live. Do they know their address? Who lives in their home? Ask them to draw a picture of their home with the people who live there. They should add their name to their picture.

- On another piece of paper of the same size as their picture ask them to paint a door. And put the number of their home on it. The door is then cut out on three sides so that it will open. The door is attached to the picture so that, when opened, it reveals the family that lives there.

- Make a group of these pictures into a display with the title 'Who lives here?' Open the doors to find out.

Where do we live?

The Seasons

Which season do you like the most?

What is it like in spring?

Spring

Where do you like to play when it is sunny?

by Lotti Christopher

When is your birthday?

What do the trees look like in autumn?

What do you like to do when it is raining?

WINTER

Wycombe Weather

Do you know where you live?

Scotland

Northern Ireland

Wales

England

What is the name of your town?

Things to do

What do you wear in the summer when it is hot?

What do you wear in the winter when it is cold?

HAVING FUN

HAVING FU

How many shops c think of?

Activities

Using the environment

✋ Count how many doors of each colour there are on a building or in a street.

✋ Do a traffic count identifying colours or types of vehicles passing the building or those found in the car park.

✋ Use a range of methods to count and display the results. Counting methods could include making a mark on paper or a small chalk or white board, simple tallying, counting aloud and tape recording the voice, using cubes or counters.

Asking questions

Who lives here?

Who lives at number...?

How many people live at number...?

In which house do most people live?

Which house has the smallest family?

Which is your home?

✋ Results may be displayed using pictograms, bar charts, computer generated graphs or 3D models.

✋ Go for a walk in the local area and take photographs to put into a class street book.

✋ Make a class collage which shows the route you took and where the photographs were taken.

✋ Make up a story of numbers in the street.

✋ Ask children to draw a picture of themselves and put in a display of the type of road they live in e.g. road, street, drive, lane

Home Links

Ask parents to:

● Look at the names of the roads and the numbers on buildings with their child when they are out and about.

● Help their child draw three buildings they pass on the way to school.

ROAD		STREET	DRIVE	LANE
😀 😀		😀	😀	

The world where we live

LEARNING INTENTIONS

Children will:

- understand that the local area is part of a region;
- know the country in which they live;
- be aware of the wider world;
- recognise different scale maps;
- know that people pollute their environment.

YOU WILL NEED

- waste materials such as paper, cardboard boxes, tubes, fabric
- paint
- coloured paper
- Aerial photograph of the school
- globe
- map of the country
- map of the world

STARTING POINTS

- Talk with the children sensitively and at an appropriate level about some environmental issues. Introduce new vocabulary such as recycle, danger, smoke, waste, pollution.

- Encourage the children to ask their own questions and show care and concern for the environment.

Where do we live?

Factory

What jobs do people do?

Hospital

Doctor

Where do we play?

Paramedic

Nurse

Traffic Warden

Where do people work?

We Live in

High Street

Shops

Shop Assistant

Where do we shop?

Office

Policeman

High Wycombe

Teacher

Playground

Postman

Fire-fighter

Town Centre

Supermarket

Activities

- Ask the children to make models out of some of the waste material you have collected.

- Make a Recycling display with the children's models.

- Talk about places they have been outside the locality including when they have travelled to other countries to visit relatives or for holidays.

- Use the world map to identify places they know or know of because of TV for example.

- Use arrows to link their display of the locality to

  - the region

  - the country

  - to the continent

  - the globe

Home Links

Encourage parents to collect paper, bottles, and cans and take them to a recycling depot.

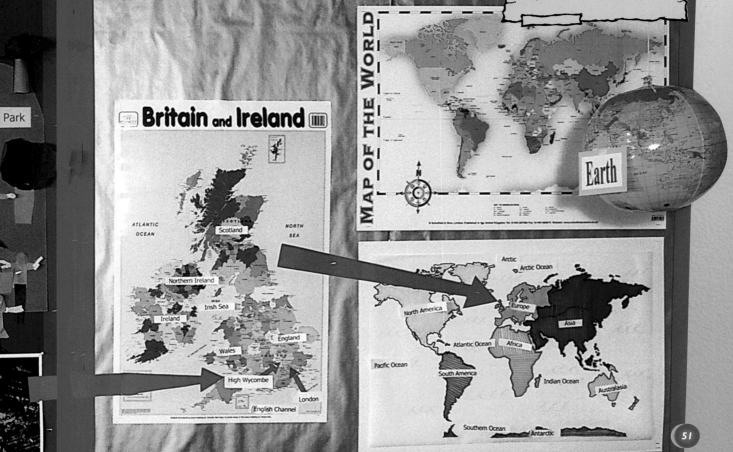

Where in the world?

LEARNING INTENTIONS

Children will:

- look at a globe and countries of the world;

- increase their awareness of crafts and traditions in their own and other cultures;

- explore and use natural and manufactured materials in an imaginative and creative way.

First Atlas

¡Challenge!
Look at the globe and the atlas
Can you find Great Britain?
Which country is to the South of Great Britain?
Which ocean is to the west of Great Britain?

STARTING POINTS

- Listen to a talk or watch a video about a visit to another country. Talk about the customs which are special to that country.

- Provide a range of artefacts or toys from different parts of the world that are made from different materials.

- Provide examples of nursery, school, village or town signs. Make a school sign; this could be small or large as the one below.

- Provide atlases, globes and photographs for the children to look at.

Activities

Patterns and Signs

In some countries, for example in India, patterns are drawn on the floor outside the door to welcome people into homes. Ask children to design and make their own 'welcome to our class' patterns. These could be made on paper using a range of materials or made in sand or drawn with chalks on paving stones or on washable floor surfaces.

Welcome

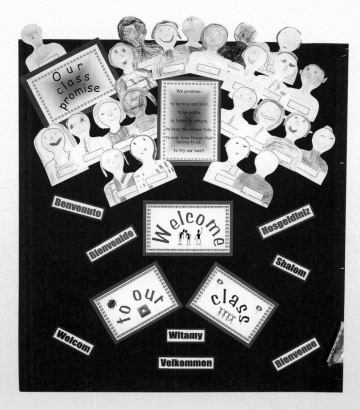

✋ Provide examples of gifts which are presented to visitors when they arrive in some places, such as a welcome garland or a hair decoration. Provide the materials for children to make their own versions.

✋ Ask children to design and make a gift they would like to give to a visitor to their class. The examples below are of necklaces the children have made.

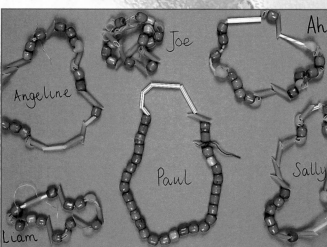

✋ Make labels for an artefact display. These could include the names of the artefacts, their country or place of origin, the material they are made from or what they are used for.

✋ Play a game with a set of artefacts, for example one where an adult gives clues without naming the object; children guess what is being described. Another game could involve removing one or two objects from a set of artefacts and the children work out what is missing.

Home Links

● Ask parents to find things in the home which have been made or bought in other countries and talk to their children about them.

● Collect postcards from different places. If parents go on holiday ask them to send the class a postcard.

Where should we go?

Activities

- Introduce children to a character such as a toy bear who is to go on holiday.
- Bring in or make a case for the clothes and other items to be taken.
- Show a map and tickets for travelling.
- Children try to work out where the bear is going from the objects e.g., a hot or cold place.
- Talk about where he or she is going and ask questions such as: *'How will he or she get to …?'* *'What will he do there?'* *'What does she need to pack?'*
- Children bring in their own toy with a small bag or case already packed.
- Friends then ask questions to discover the destination.

TALK ABOUT

Questions to ask	Language development
Where is he going?	Names of places.
How will she get there?	Types of transport.
What will he do there?	Different activities.
What does she need to take?	Clothes, phrase book, sun creams etc.
What type of money will he need?	Introduce different currencies.

Activities

- Children select a place on a globe or map of Europe or the World. Describe the things they might see or experience on a journey to that place.

- Display postcards around a map. The example below is of Europe but this could be of one country or another continent.

- Ask and answer questions about the postcards and the countries they are from.

- Display dolls from different countries in traditional costumes. Talk about how traditional dress is different from the ordinary clothes people wear and the reasons people wear traditional costumes.

Faraway places

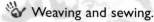

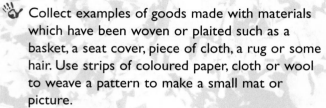

Activities

✋ Weaving and sewing.

✋ Collect examples of goods made with materials which have been woven or plaited such as a basket, a seat cover, piece of cloth, a rug or some hair. Use strips of coloured paper, cloth or wool to weave a pattern to make a small mat or picture.

✋ Provide a set of simple outline pictures of photographs cut from magazines or old calendars which have been laminated. Punch holes at regular intervals. Ask children to sew these with large blunt needles or laces, choosing appropriate colours. Ask questions about the pictures which may show features of the natural and made environment such as a hill, river, house, car.

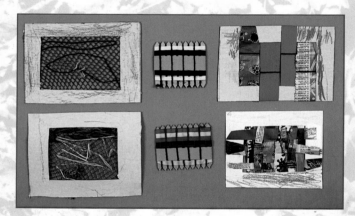

✋ Collect pictures of distant places from calendars, post cards, greeting cards, magazines, or download from the internet.

TALK ABOUT

Questions to ask

What does this picture show?

Where is it?

What are the people doing?

What do you like / dislike about this place?

Language development

Encourage the children to:

name features

describe activities

pass opinions.

Activities

- Make an artefact display.

- Make labels. These could include the names of the objects, the place they come from, the materials they are made of and what they are used for.

- Play a game with a set of artefacts. The adult gives clues without naming the object. Children guess what it is. Another game could involve removing one or two objects from the display and the children work out what is missing.

- Make a huge display of a distant place. The example shown below is of a rainforest but it could be a desert, the banks of the River Nile, a tropical beach.

- Encourage children to use appropriate vocabulary to describe the features.

- Talk about the similarities and differences of the places they know.

- Ask children to paint giant leaf shapes, suspend these from the ceiling or on the collage

- Hang these at different heights and talk about which is the highest / lowest, biggest / smallest.

We found out about rainforests

lovely magical valuable wonderful special beautiful

STORYBOX
...VING THE ...NFORESTS
DESERTS AND RAINFORESTS
THE GREAT GREEN FOREST
Paul Geraghty

Jobs people do

LEARNING INTENTIONS

Children will:

- take part in role-play with confidence and increasing understanding;

- develop their awareness of the jobs people do and the activities people engage in both within and beyond their experience;

- experience a range of cultures and investigate similarities and differences.

YOU WILL NEED

- pictures of people doing different jobs

- dressing up clothes representing a variety of occupations

- toy figures

STARTING POINTS

- Provide a set of toy figures doing various jobs and talk about the clothes they are wearing and the jobs they do.

- Show pictures which demonstrate people doing different jobs such as the police or farmers.

- Introduce vocabulary such as job, work, uniform, special clothes.

- Invite in a visitor such as a firefighter or a chef to talk to the children about the work they do.

- Read a story or an information book that is about work people do. This could be factual or fictional such as 'The Jolly Postman'; or 'The Lighthouse Keeper's Lunch'.

Activities

Using dressing up clothes

Use your collection of dressing up clothes and equipment to form a display.

Ensure the clothes reflect a range of jobs which can be role-played by both sexes.

Role play: doctors and nurses

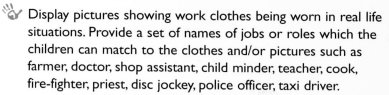

Display pictures showing work clothes being worn in real life situations. Provide a set of names of jobs or roles which the children can match to the clothes and/or pictures such as farmer, doctor, shop assistant, child minder, teacher, cook, fire-fighter, priest, disc jockey, police officer, taxi driver.

The children can choose freely which role they wish to assume or the teacher can direct them to a certain role and ask the children to select the appropriate item or items to wear or use. Provide a full-length mirror at child height to encourage discussion.

Adults can participate in the role-play and model behaviour and language which the children learn from.

Put a selection of picture books near the dressing up clothes to give children ideas for play. Change these regularly.

Asking questions

Who wears this?

What is this used for?

Where might I see this?

What would I do with this?

What work does this person do?

Role play: fishing

Home Links

- Ask children to bring in pictures from magazines or books to add to the collection of people working in another country.

- Ask parents and carers to talk to the children about:

  – the work they do.

  – the work people do in the places they visit e.g. leisure centre, supermarket, cinema, hospital

Role play: cafe

Role play: gardens

Role play: a Vietnamese meal

In the playground and park

LEARNING INTENTIONS

Children will:

- know more about signs and symbols and use these in free and directed play;
- follow oral and printed directions;
- be aware of why and how people can take care of the environment;
- know what people do in the park.

YOU WILL NEED

- wheeled toys
- paint
- stipple paint brushes
- paper
- paint
- straws
- glue

STARTING POINTS

- Children play on pedal cars, bicycles, trikes and other wheeled toys.
- Children play in an open space, playground or park.
- Talk about the children's experiences of visiting parks.

- Read the children a story or a poem such as 'After the Storm'. Use the book to introduce new vocabulary for example *storm, wind, fence, tree, branch, roots, stream, bridge, lake, acorn*.

Activities

Signs and symbols

- Talk about and make some symbols that children already know such as stop, go, no entry, traffic lights, pedestrian crossing. Children can use these in outdoor play activities.

- Make sets of cards with directions for children to use in the playground such as symbols, arrows, numerals and number symbols.

- Make cards for children to follow a route around the large apparatus. These may use words and phrases such as; *go under, climb over, walk through* or you may use picture clues, which the children have already been taught.

Activities

- Devise with the children a 'Code of conduct in the park'.

- Make a list (teacher may scribe) of ways children can improve the park environment. Talk about putting litter in bins, not picking flowers, not pulling on branches, the importance of playing in safe places.

- Make a class collage of 'Fun in the park'. Children can paint pictures of activities they can do in the park or of features they might find there.

- Children can make 3-D models of park playground furniture with straws.

- Children can make mosaic type pictures by using paint and a stipple technique.

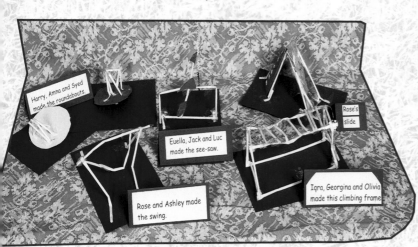

Harry, Amna and Syed made the roundabouts.

Euella, Jack and Luc made the see-saw.

Rose's slide

Rose and Ashley made the swing.

Iqra, Georgina and Olivia made this climbing frame.

Home Links

Ask parents to:

- Look with their children for signs and symbols in the environment and to explain their meaning.

- Visit a local park and help their child draw pictures of what they did there.

Action songs and rhymes

LEARNING INTENTIONS

Children will:

- begin to understand that they are singing and talking about songs and rhymes that relate to the world around them;

- ask and answer questions;

- develop an awareness of environmental issues.

In all cases it is expected that you would sing the song a number of times so the children become familiar with it.

- Sing action songs and rhymes that relate to the real world.

- Use something which the children have created which relates to a song or rhyme such as a bus for 'The wheels on the bus go round and round' or the log and pool scene for 'Five little speckled frogs' or the pan and sausages for 'Ten fat sausages'.

Five Little Ducks

- Make a picture to show where the ducks went.

- Make ducks to move around the picture. These can be given names or letters or numbers and used for word, letter and number recognition.

- Cut out duck shapes from card for the children to decorate with material, paper, feathers.

- Punch holes in the shapes for threading or sewing.

- Provide a set of laminated labels for the children to attach to the picture in the right place using Blutack or Velcro pieces. These could include:

  - *over the hills*
  - *up the hill*
  - *along the path*
  - *through the wood*
  - *across the river*
  - *in the water.*
  - *over the stepping stones*

- Talk about what the ducks would see, what they would pass, what food they would eat, who they would meet.

- Ask questions such as: 'If you went swimming, where would you go? What would you wear?' 'Why must you be careful near water?'

> One little duck went swimming one day over the hills and far away, He was having so much fun he asked another one to come.
> Two little ducks went swimming one day ....

Five little speckled frogs

> Five little speckled frogs
> sat on a speckled log
> eating a most enormous grub
> YUM YUM
> One fell into the pool
> where it was nice and cool
> then there were four speckled frogs
> GLUB GLUB
> Four little speckled frogs
> sat on a speckled log
> eating.......

5 little speckled frogs

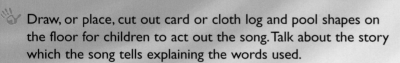

1
2
3
4
5

- Draw, or place, cut out card or cloth log and pool shapes on the floor for children to act out the song. Talk about the story which the song tells explaining the words used.

- Make a collage picture of the scene for the five speckled frogs. Use cut out frogs or felt frog finger puppets for the children to move as appropriate.

- Talk about the different environments and habitats which may surround the log and the pool. Introduce vocabulary such as mud, stones, reeds. Ask children to imagine what it would feel like to be in the different locations such as: 'in the pool' 'on the log' 'under the stone' 'in the mud' 'among the reeds'.

- Make a cardboard wheel with a spinner to use with your collage picture. Divide the wheel into sections with an instruction such as 'put one frog in the mud' in each section. Children take turns to spin and follow the instruction.

Home Links

- Send home a list of words which have been introduced as new vocabulary and ask parents to use these, where possible, in general conversations with their child.

- Look for examples of some of the words such as wall, bus, star, hill, log. Draw a picture of one of them.

Compass Town (Page 47)